© 2012 by Barbour Publishing, Inc.

Compiled by Kathryn Deering in association with Snapdragon Group℠, Tulsa, OK.

ISBN 978-1-61626-612-7

All rights reserved. No part of this publication may be reproduced or transmitted for commercial purposes, except for brief quotations in printed reviews, without written permission of the publisher.

Published by Barbour Publishing, Inc., P.O. Box 719, Uhrichsville, Ohio 44683, www.barbourbooks.com

Our mission is to publish and distribute inspirational products offering exceptional value and biblical encouragement to the masses.

Printed in China.

A Little Book of tweets

for GRADS

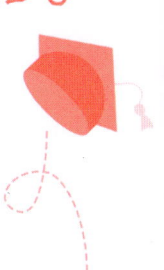

"2 succeed in life,
u need 3 things:
a wishbone, a backbone,
& a funnybone."
—Unknown

Faced with the necessity of applying 4 jobs. Suddenly, downloading new music takes precedence.
#Welcome2TheRealWorld

"The only way of finding the limits of the possible is by going beyond them into the impossible."
—Arthur C. Clarke

Spent $60 on my cap & gown. Wore them once. Now trying 2 figure out another use 4 them. Nightgown & cheese tray? Not so easy.

"Make ur life a mission, not an intermission."
—Arnold H. Glasow

Just figured out that Dad was right: $ doesn't grow on trees. Bummer. #Welcome2TheRealWorld

Some days I can't think except in music lyrics. Speaking of which, I think it's time 2 buy more music!

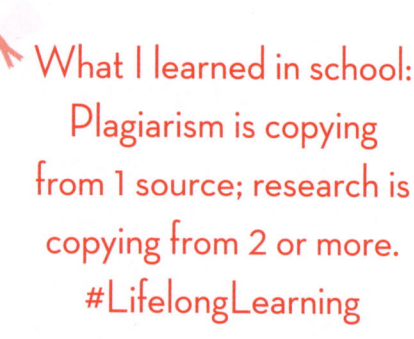

What I learned in school: Plagiarism is copying from 1 source; research is copying from 2 or more. #LifelongLearning

"There r so many difficulties in the way...but I keep on trying, knowing that perseverance & patience win in the end."
—Helen Keller

This whole living-on-ur-own thing has its pros & cons. Pro: No curfew. Con: Gotta buy my own toilet paper. #Welcome2TheRealWorld

I think this quote was written about me & my friends: "The greatest oak was once a little nut that held its ground."

Babysitting win: Eating from a barrel of cheese balls & watching Disney. #StillAKid@<3

#GraduationWin:
Never having 2 ask a parent 2 sign a grade card again!

"U HAVE BRAINS IN UR HEAD.
U HAVE FEET IN UR SHOES.
U CAN STEER URSELF IN
ANY DIRECTION U CHOOSE."
—DR. SEUSS

Saw this on a license plate:
Graduate Soon! Millions on
Welfare Depend on U!

#GraduationWin:
No more hall passes!

Well said, Mr. Twain!
"I have never let my schooling interfere with my education."
—Mark Twain

#SavvyGradSays:
"Every day when I wake up, I realize I have my whole life ahead of me. Now's the time 2 make decisions & make them good."

Good-byes r not 4ever.
Good-byes r not the end.
They simply mean I'll miss
u until we meet again!

"Commencement speeches—
invented in the belief that
students should never b
released. . .until they've
been properly sedated."
—G. Trudeau

"UR GOALS R THE ROAD MAPS THAT GUIDE U & SHOW U WHAT IS POSSIBLE 4 UR LIFE."
—LES BROWN

"I HONESTLY THINK IT IS BETTER 2 B A FAILURE @ SOMETHING U LUV THAN 2 B A SUCCESS @ SOMETHING U HATE."

—GEORGE BURNS

"Take it from some1 who knows. It's really embarrassing during ur commencement when u yawn & swallow ur tassel."
—Joe Hickman

#SavvyGradSays: "Seriously, what's with the robes & flat hats? We wouldn't b caught dead dressed like this anyplace else."

RT@MOM: "U R AMAZING! ALL THESE YRS OF WORK PAID OFF IN A BIG WAY! THE SKY IS THE LIMIT NOW. THERE'S NOTHING HOLDING U BACK!"

#SavvyGradSays:
"Hey world, get ready 2 get ur socks knocked off by this yr's grads. 2day is our day."

Dear God, thnks 4 setting in my <3 the desire 2 set & achieve goals. Graduation is a big 1. Pls show me what's next. Amen.

"The doors we open & close each day decide the lives we live."
—Flora Whittemore

Found some elementary school projects the other day. Brought back some fun memories & made me want 2 do arts & crafts!
#StillAKid@<3

Shout out 2 my buds:
"School's out, memories past, don't ever doubt our friendship will last."
—Unknown

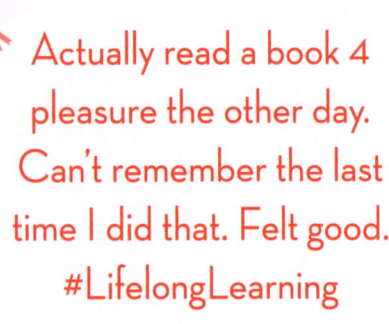

Actually read a book 4 pleasure the other day. Can't remember the last time I did that. Felt good. #LifelongLearning

"Destiny is not a matter of chance; it is a matter of choice."
—William Jennings Bryan

"May u live all the days of ur life."
—Jonathan Swift

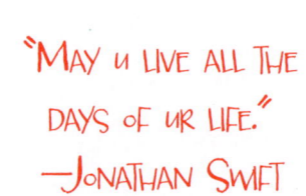

#GraduationWin: We've got enuf leftovers from the grad party that I won't have 2 buy lunch 4 a solid 6 months.

"Nothing happens unless first a dream."
—Carl Sandburg

"4get mistakes. 4get failure. 4get everything except what u're going 2 do now & do it."
—Will Durant

Job interviews: exciting, nerve racking, terrifying, fun—all @ the same time. Kind of like a roller coaster.
#Welcome2TheRealWorld

#SavvyGradSays:
"Appreciate the ppl in ur life. Time of exciting change is in ur future, & relationships r what can keep u grounded."

"May ur dreams defy
the laws of gravity."
—H. Jackson Brown Jr.

"HAPPINESS IS THE REAL SENSE OF FULFILLMENT THAT COMES FROM HARD WORK."
—JOSEPH BARBARA

I WAS IN SENIORITIS MODE 4 SO MANY MONTHS, IT'S BEEN HARD 2 PULL OUT OF IT. BUT I MUST! #Welcome2TheRealWorld

"1 way 2 get the most out of life is 2 look upon it as an adventure."
—William Feather

As the end of school came near, I was so ready 2 get out of there! Now I'm kind of missing the everydayness of it all.

#GraduationWin:
Deposited my grad gifts into the bank. Never seen so many digits in my account total! I am blessed.

It's just smart: b4 I leave a burger place, I always refill my soft drink in case the next Great Depression hits as soon as I step outside.

"The best thing about the future is that it comes only 1 day @ a time."
—Abraham Lincoln

"The future belongs 2 those who believe in the beauty of their dreams."
—Eleanor Roosevelt

#LifelongLearning:
"What we become depends on what we read after all of the professors have finished with us."
—Thomas Carlyle

#GraduationWin: No more homework, no more books! No more teachers' dirty looks! (Which I got a lot of...)

#SavvyGradSays: "Reputation is what u need 2 get a job. Character is what u need 2 keep it."

"Many of life's failures r ppl who did not realize how close they were 2 success when they gave up."
—Thomas Edison

I just filled up my car with gas. Now it's worth @ least $50.
#Welcome2TheRealWorld

"U R SUCCESSFUL THE MOMENT U START MOVING TOWARD A WORTHWHILE GOOD."
—CHARLES CARLSON

All this change in my life right now makes me thnkful 4 the constants: my family, faith, & friends.

"The world is round & the place which may seem like the end may also b only the beginning."
—George Baker

"2 SUCCEED, U NEED 2 TAKE THAT GUT FEELING IN WHAT U BELIEVE & ACT ON IT WITH ALL OF UR <3."
—CHRISTY BORGELD

#SavvyGradSays:
"Fall seven times, stand up eight" (Japanese Proverb).

I thought after graduation I'd have all kinds of time on my hands 2 do whatever I want. I was wrong. #Welcome2TheRealWorld

I recently started watching science documentaries on DVD. I guess I miss physics class. Who knew? #LifelongLearning

"Education is the most powerful weapon, which u can use 2 change the world."
—Nelson Mandela

Hold on 2 ur hats, folks!
"The best way 2 prepare 4
life is 2 begin 2 live."
—Elbert Hubbard

Wise words, indeed: "If ur parents never had children, chances r u won't either."
—Dick Cavett

"The best way 2 predict the future is 2 invent it."
—Alan Kay

#SavvyGradSays:
"OUT OF SCHOOL—GROWING SMARTER BY DEGREES."

"OBSTACLES R THINGS A PERSON SEES WHEN HE TAKES HIS EYES OFF HIS GOAL."
—E. JOSEPH COSSMAN

Here's an adult lesson learned (the hard way): don't mix reds & whites in the laundry—unless u like the color pink!

"WHATEVER U R, B A GOOD 1."
—ABRAHAM LINCOLN

#LifelongLearning:
"The student who graduates 2day & stops learning 2morrow is uneducated the day after."
—Newton D. Baker

"A professor is 1 who talks in some1 else's sleep."
—W. H. Auden

"IN THE MIDDLE OF EVERY
DIFFICULTY LIES OPPORTUNITY."
—ALBERT EINSTEIN

I've eaten a lot of Ramen over the yrs—so much that sometimes I now crave it!

The real world has this weird way of being so... real. I'm ready 2 go back 2 second grade! Who's with me?
#Welcome2TheRealWorld

Life lesson #68: Used my debit card 4 a cup of coffee, overdrew, & incurred a $35 overdraft fee. Always know ur balance!

"If u can imagine it,
u can achieve it.
If u can dream it,
u can become it."
—William Arthur Ward

God, thnk U 4 the talents & abilities U have given 2 me. Pls show me how I can use them 2 glorify U. Amen.

#SavvyGradSays:
"There r times we all feel overwhelmed. Take a deep breath. With God's help, u'll make it thru."

"Take the first step in faith. U don't have 2 see the whole staircase, just take the first step."
—Martin Luther King Jr.

#GraduationWin: It was wonderful 2 have family & friends come 2 visit during grad celebrations. Luv u guys!

"It is more fun 2 talk with some1 who doesn't use long, difficult words but rather short, easy words, like what about lunch?"
—Winnie the Pooh

Updating my résumé. Do u think I can list babysitting as "executive childcare manager"? Might b a stretch. #Welcome2TheRealWorld

"If @ first u don't succeed,
find out if the loser
gets anything."
—Bill Lyon

Life lesson #87:
Duct tape can b used
2 fix anything—really!

"Talk happiness; talk faith; talk health. Say u r well, & all is well with u, & God shall hear ur words."
—Ella Wheeler Wilcox

Still updating my résumé. How about listing mowing yards as "professional horticultural specialist"? 2 much? #Welcome2TheRealWorld

#SavvyGradSays:
"No matter what u're going thru, u're not the only 1 going thru it."

"THINGS R NEVER QUITE AS SCARY WHEN U HAVE A BEST FRIEND."
—BILL WATTERSON

I NEVER FULLY APPRECIATED THE IDEA OF "WORKING 4 THE WEEKEND" UNTIL I GOT MY FIRST FULL-TIME JOB. <3 FRIDAYS! #Welcome2TheRealWorld

Went back 2 my alma mater 4 a visit. Y does every1 look so young? (& y do I feel so old?) #StillAKid@<3

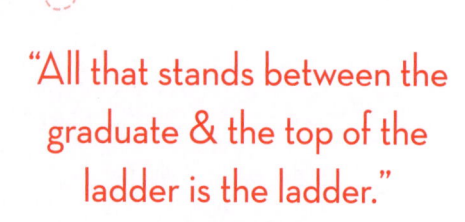

"All that stands between the graduate & the top of the ladder is the ladder."
—Unknown

"America believes in education: the average professor earns more $ in a yr than a pro athlete earns in a whole week."

—Evan Esar

I wish I were a speed reader. Think of all the time I could've saved in school! (Or maybe I would've actually read the assignments!)

"Do what u can, with what u have, where u r."
—Teddy Roosevelt

#SavvyGradSays:
"The tassel is worth the hassle!"

"NOTHING TAKES THE TASTE OUT OF PEANUT BUTTER QUITE LIKE UNREQUITED LUV."
—CHARLES M. SCHULZ

Even Hippocrates had a lazy bone: "2 do nothing is sometimes a good remedy."

I'm taking responsibility 4 my own learning. I will learn how 2 beat this video game, & I won't stop till it's done!
#StillAKid@<3

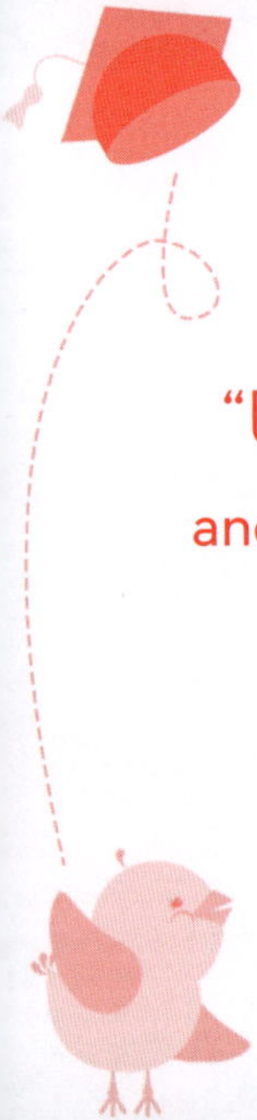

"U r never 2 old 2 set another goal or 2 dream a new dream."
—C. S. Lewis

"Rule #1: use ur good judgment in all situations. There will b no additional rules."
—Nordstrom Employee Handbook

"The road 2 success is always under construction."
—Lily Tomlin

Got a call 4 a second interview 4 a job I really want. I've got something like first-date jitters! #Welcome2TheRealWorld

There's a lot of responsibility that comes with being an adult. But on the upside, u can have ice cream 4 lunch if that's what u want!

"WITHOUT ICE CREAM THERE WOULD B DARKNESS & CHAOS."
—DON KARDONG

"The future is not something we enter. The future is something we create."

—Unknown

"Believe deep down in ur <3 that u're destined 2 do great things."
—Joe Paterno

I will never understand y I resisted naps as a child. I'd kill 4 1 right now. #Welcome2TheRealWorld

"The great pleasure in life is doing what ppl say u cannot do."
—Walter Bagehot

Life lesson #98: Don't go grocery shopping when u're hungry. Oy ve. So much junk food!

"The commencement speaker tells students dressed in identical caps & gowns that individuality is the key 2 success."
—Robert Orben

Thinking about signing up 4 a class just bcuz I want 2...not bcuz I have 2! #LifelongLearning

2day I am celebrating
little accomplishments—
like the fact that I sent out
25 résumés b4 lunch!

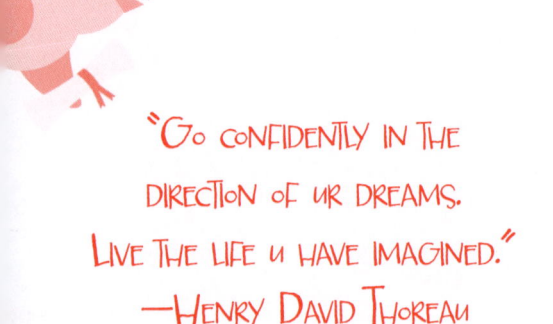

"Go confidently in the direction of ur dreams. Live the life u have imagined."
—Henry David Thoreau

#GraduationWin:
With all the graduation parties I've been going 2, I haven't had 2 plan a meal in 2 whole weeks!

#SavvyGradSays:
"Live without pretending.
Luv without depending.
Listen without defending.
Speak without offending."

"2 accomplish great things, we must not only act, but also dream; not only plan, but also believe."
—Anatole France

Learning this more every day: "Kind words do not cost much. Yet they accomplish much."

—Blaise Pascal

"Don't bunt.
Aim out of the ballpark."
—David Ogilvy

#SavvyGradSays: "Education was good 4 me. I'm starting 2 understand how my parents tick. B4 I just tried 2 avoid ticking them off."

I know my friends & family have my best interest @ <3, but if 1 more person asks me what my plans r, I might just lose it. (Pray 4 me.)

INDIGENCE (N.):
A CONDITION OF EXTREME POVERTY OR DESTITUTION; PENURY, NEEDINESS (I.E., URS TRULY).

"I couldn't wait 4 success,
so I went ahead without it."
—Jonathan Winters

My education has made me think about things in a new way, like, what if there were no hypothetical questions?
#LifelongLearning

Here's another question my educated mind wants 2 know: Do vegetarians eat animal crackers?

"A dream doesn't become reality thru magic; it takes sweat, determination, & hard work."
—Colin Powell

"LIFE IS MY COLLEGE.
MAY I GRADUATE WELL
& EARN SOME HONORS!"
—LOUISA MAY ALCOTT

LIFE LESSON #154:
WAIT UNTIL U GET UR FIRST PAYCHECK 2 SEE HOW MUCH $ U'RE ACTUALLY MAKING.
TAXES. OUCH.

Dear God, U have put so many opportunities within my reach! Help me 2 see them as blessings instead of burdens 2day & every day. Amen.

"IDEAS R LIKE RABBITS.
U GET A COUPLE & LEARN HOW
2 HANDLE THEM, & PRETTY
SOON U HAVE A DOZEN."
—JOHN STEINBECK

#SavvyGradSays:
"Success comes in cans;
failure in can'ts."

No matter how old I get & how much of an adult I become, home will always b home 2 me. #StillAKid@<3

"The best educated human being is the 1 who understands most about the life in which he is placed."
—Helen Keller

"If u think education is expensive, try ignorance."
—Derek Bok

Now I understand y
my parents complained
about the mail...
It's all bills, bills, bills!
#Welcome2TheRealWorld

My day began with a heaping bowl of Fruity Pebbles. I feel it's only right 2 end it that way as well. #StillAKid@<3

"There r 2 kinds of perfect:
the 1 u can never achieve
& the other, by just
being urself."
—Lauren King

"The time is always right
2 do what is right."
—Martin Luther King Jr.

#SavvyGradSays:
"Laughter is an everyday necessity. Don't let any1 tell u otherwise."

"It takes courage 2 grow up & become who u really r."
—E. E. Cummings

"Don't tell me the sky's the limit when there r footsteps on the moon."
—Unknown

"[Diplomas] make pretty good placemats if u get 'em laminated."
—Jeph Jacques